Frank A. Hildebrand, Theodore Bland Noss

**The Seventh School Year**

A course of study for pupils of the seventh grade

Frank A. Hildebrand, Theodore Bland Noss

**The Seventh School Year**
*A course of study for pupils of the seventh grade*

ISBN/EAN: 9783337780340

Printed in Europe, USA, Canada, Australia, Japan

Cover: Foto ©Paul-Georg Meister /pixelio.de

More available books at **www.hansebooks.com**

Normal Help Series, No. VII.

# The Seventh School Year.

## A Course of Study
## For Pupils of the Seventh Grade.

PREPARED FOR THE
USE OF TEACHERS AND FOR USE IN NORMAL AND
TRAINING SCHOOL CLASSES.

### By F. Alonzo Hildebrand,

Training Teacher for the Seventh Grade, State Normal School,
California, Pa.

THEO. B. NOSS, General Editor.

Published by the
STATE NORMAL SCHOOL,
CALIFORNIA. PA.

# Preface.

In preparing this course of study, it has not been the intention to give in full detail all of the work, but to give a general idea of *some* of the work that the author thinks desirable in a course of study for the seventh year of a child's school life.

While this work has been prepared especially for the Practice Department of the State Normal School at California, Pa., the author sees no reason why the same course might not be successfully used in other schools of like grade.

It has been the constant aim to keep in mind the advantage of correlations of material. History has here been made the basis, and, as far as possible, other studies have been correlated with it. The way has not always been clear nor the task easy. Imperfect as it may be, the author presents this course of study in the hope that it may prove helpful to teachers.                                                        F. A. H.

## CONSPECTUS OF SE

| I. SCIENCE. | | II. HISTORY AND LITER | |
|---|---|---|---|
| **GEOGRAPHY.** | **NATURE STUDY.** | **U. S. HISTORY.** | **LITI** |
| NORTH AMERICA.<br>Eastern Coast.<br>West Indies.<br>Atlantic Ocean.<br>Mexico. | A study of 25 common weeds. | Condition of Europe at the close of XVth Century<br>Columbus<br>Spanish and English Discoveries<br>Early Races in America | Ulysses and<br>Voyage of Co<br>The Indians<br>Conquest of : |
| NORTH AMERICA.<br>Appalachian Highland<br>Mississippi River Basin<br>Great Lakes<br>St. Lawrence Valley | Study of leaves<br>Blue Prints | French and Dutch Discoveries<br>Claims of the four nations<br>Maps of discoveries | "La Salle an<br>Great Lakes."<br>"The Paper ( |
| NORTH AMERICA.<br>Western Highland<br>Prairies and Plains<br>Review Relief Forms<br>Relief Maps | Collection of Nuts | SETTLEMENTS<br>Virginia<br>Massachusetts<br>Connecticut<br>Rhode Island<br>New Hampshire | "Courtship o<br>"First Landi<br>"The Mayflo<br>"The Phanto<br>Washington"<br>"Beyond the |
| U.S. { Government<br>Climate<br>Products<br>Grouping of States<br>Special study of each group<br>Product maps | ROCKS<br>Vermont rocks<br>Hudson River cliffs<br>Pennsylvania rocks<br>Rock collection | SETTLEMENTS<br>New York<br>New Jersey<br>Pennsylvania<br>Delaware, Maryland<br>Carolinas, Georgia | Irving's Kul<br>of New York<br>"Van Rensse<br>wick"—Brook<br>"Historic Bo<br>Study of Irvi |
| British America<br>Alaska—Central America<br>Review Mexico<br>Maps of distances<br>Correlate History | Study of the Moon. | Inter-Colonial Wars<br>King William's<br>Queen Anne's<br>King George's<br>French and Indian<br>Colonial Civilization | "The Old R<br>Parkman<br>"Evangeline<br>"Montcalm a<br>Lady Yeardl |
| SOUTH AMERICA.<br>Reliefs<br>Selvas, Llanos, Pampas<br>Eastern Highland | Study of the stars<br>Location of fifteen constellations<br>Myths about stars | Revolu-<br>tionary<br>War { 1 Action around Boston<br>2 Washington to Morristown<br>3 Washington from Morristown to Valley Forge<br>4 Burgoyne 5 Greene | "The Spy"—<br>"Declaration<br>Grandmothei<br>Hill<br>Paul Revere'<br>Study of Lon |
| SOUTH AMERICA.<br>Countries. Government<br>Climate. People<br>Products<br>Map Studies<br>Political changes | Study of the sun | NATIONAL DEVELOPMENT<br>Articles of Confederation<br>Constitution<br>Washington's Administration<br>John Adam's Administration<br>Jefferson's Administration | "Washington<br>Life of Wash<br>Study of Whi<br>Boy Travelei<br>Voyage arou<br>wla |
| EUROPE<br>Position, Form, Reliefs,<br>Countries, Government,<br>Climate, Industries | CLOUDS<br>Formation<br>Kinds<br>Experimental electricity, leading to the spark<br>Lightning | Madison's Administration<br>War of 1812 { On Land<br>{ On Water | Perry's Victc<br>Study of<br>Shakespeare<br>"The Voice c<br>"April Day" |
| EUROPE<br>For special study:<br>England, German Empire, France, and Mediterranean Countries<br>Correlate History and Literature<br>Product and Distance Maps | Practical experiments with oxygen | Monroe's Administration<br>J. Q. Adams<br>Internal Improvements<br>Review of Slavery and Finance up to 1820. | "Bingen on t<br>Extracts fro<br>and Michael At<br>"Greece"—B<br>"Arabs in Sp |

| TURE. | III. NUMBERS. | IV. LANGUAGE. | V. ARTS. |
|---|---|---|---|
| ITURE. | ARITHMETIC. | ENGLISH. | WRITING=MUSIC. |
| nbus jus co | Common Fractions<br>Questions of Distance and Area<br>Actual measurements<br>Constructing Plots | Synthesis<br>Noun, Pronoun and Verb<br>Composition work based upon History and Literature | Vertical Writing—Daily<br>Songs:<br>"Annie Laurie"<br>"Grandmother's Chair"<br>Drawing—sketching |
| Discovery of the kman 9" | MEASUREMENTS<br>Tables—Linear and Square<br>Carpeting<br>Plastering<br>Painting | Synthesis<br>Adjective and Adjective Phrases<br>Adverb and Adv. Phrases<br>Conjunction and Preposition<br>Composition based on Geography and History. | Vertical Writing—Daily<br>Songs:<br>"October's Party"<br>"The Little Brown Church" |
| es Standish" the Pilgrims"<br>tip" [clamation anksgiving Pro· cies"—Stoddard | MEASUREMENTS<br>Volumes, Tables<br>Contents of Bins<br>Irregularly shaped Vessels<br>Area of Circle · ·a<br>Capacity of Cylinder | Properties of the Parts of Speech<br>Interjection<br>Analysis of Simple Sentences<br>Paraphrasing of selections in History | Vertical Writing<br>Memorizing of Common Hymns<br>Drawing—Nature |
| bocker's History<br>of Rensselaers· | MEASUREMENTS<br>Weight—Avoirdupois, Troy, and Apothecary<br>Time Measure<br>Practical Work in Reduction of Denominate Numbers | Careful drill on Verbs and Pronouns<br>Analysis of Simple Sentences<br>Composition | Vertical Writing<br>Study of Raphael Madonnas<br>Songs:<br>"Flow Gently Sweet Afton"<br>"Merry Christmas"<br>Drawing |
| e in Canada"—<br>/olfe"—Parkman uost. | Drill in Denominate Numbers<br>Short Processes<br>Review of Longitude and Time<br>Correlate with work in Geography | Verb "to be"<br>Perfect Tense<br>Noun Clause<br>Adj. Clause<br>Adv. Clause | Vertical Writing<br>Songs:<br>"The Old Oaken Bucket"<br>"Billy Boy"<br>Drawings of Moon Phases |
| er idependence" Story of Bunker<br>le ow | 1st Processes of Percentage<br>Home applications<br>Make questions correlating with Geography work | Synthesis in Words, Phrases and Clauses<br>Analysis of Complex Sentences<br>Book Reports | Vertical Writing<br>Songs:<br>"Crowding Awfully"<br>"Marching through Georgia"<br>Maps of Constellations. |
| irewell Address"—<br>in , Andrew's Brazil Brazil<br>ne World—Dar· | Principles of Gain and Loss<br>Agents—their work<br>· ommissions, Insurance<br>Taxes and duties based upon S. A. products | Compound Sentences<br>A careful study of "Snowbound"<br>Paraphasing and Composition Work on Nature Study | Vertical Writing<br>Songs:<br>"We'ed Better Bide a Wee"<br>"Blue Bells of Scotland"<br>Drawings based upon Geography |

# COURSE OF STUDY.

## *One year in the Seventh Grade.*

# General Introduction.

The whole course of study has been divided into five groups: science, history and literature, arithmetic, language, and the arts—each having its own distinctive place in mental growth, yet uniting with the other four to promote the harmonious development of the mind.

No special place is set apart for Orthography. It can best be taught in connection with other studies.

A good working vocabulary should be built up. Choose from the day's work about twenty words to be studied for the next day. Let them be selected from the different subjects and conversation of the day. Let the pupils have blank-books specially prepared in which to keep the list as selected. Have frequent drills on the list. Spell and use in sentences. Endeavor to use the words in class and conversation as much as possible. Review fifty or more words at a time and create a rivalry for best work.

The Reading is found in the literature used in the different branches. It is not the intention to entirely ignore selections not correlated with other material. Humorous as well as other isolated selections have their value, and every careful teacher knows just when such should be read.

Teach the pupils to be rapid readers,--rapid thought getters. How many will ever be called upon for a show of fine elocution? In silent reading, see not only sentences but short paragraphs at a glance.

Special lessons will be given on Physiology during the year. This work will be done methodically, both as to time and material. Special attention will be given to hygiene and simple anatomy.

# SEPTEMBER, or First Month.

## GEOGRAPHY.

### Introduction.

The work in geography includes North America, South America, and parts of Europe. The aim is to teach as much history as possible in connection with place and condition.

Why should geography and history be taught separately, especially, during the first seven or eight years of school life? What is geography to children without people, industries and government? What is history but dealing with people? History and geography are brothers—both wearing the same shoes.

Study places from the home center; keep direction, distance, and intervening earth in mind.

Keep in the hands of the pupils books of travel, etc., such as "Boys in Other Countries," "Zig-zag Journeys," Knox's "Boy Travelers" series, and Mara Pratt's books on history and geography. All these are excellent helps.

I.   NORTH AMERICA—EASTERN COAST—
    Study the Atlantic Slope from the St. Lawrence river to the Gulf of Mexico.   Note well the courses of the rivers and situation of broken mountain ranges.   Have the entire slope sketched on the board, and have the pupils make their own on drawing paper.   Have each pupil know each river and its curves, since on this slope is based most of the history of the United States.

II.   WEST INDIES—STUDY—
    1st.   Position regarding Europe and the United States.   First require the relative then the absolute position.

2nd. Size and number of islands.
3rd. Ownership.
4th. Government.
5th. Climate—reasons.
6th. Industries—how determined—results.
7th. People—nationalities.
8th. Commerce—with whom.
Have principal islands sketched and absolute position observed.
III. ATLANTIC OCEAN—
   1. Situation.
   2. Size and shape.
   3. Its troughs.
   4. Animals.
   5. Currents.
   6. Routes of vessels.
Emphasize the troughs, and also the shore, teach harbors, necessity for the same, situation along the Atlantic coast U. S., why the large cities are so situated, advantage of currents to navigators, effect upon the climate.
IV. MEXICO—
   1. Relative and absolute position—Results { Climate. Occupations. Productions. Thrift of natives.
   2. Relative size.
   3. Surface—mountain ranges, plateaus, and plains.
   4. People—history of Mexico, languages, customs.
   5. Political Divisions—government.
   6. Cities, rivers, places of interest.
In dealing with the history, briefly outline the founding of Mexico, its independence, present government. Compare the customs with ours. Be careful in pronunciation of Spanish names, teach spelling of them.

## U. S. HISTORY AND LITERATURE.

### Introduction.

The work takes the history of the United States up to Jackson's administration. Avoid the exclusive use of a single text-book. Cling to the primary books, for after all is said, they give the pupil the best material.

Study men and their relations to the nation and you have our history. Avoid any method that suggests a committing of words. Causes and effects are grasped by children if the teacher be a good leader. Review daily—not exactly the same facts presented in the same way, but vary the method and introduce new material.

There are very few pupils that do not become interested in people,— their customs, industries, etc. Why not then grasp this vital truth and spice the whole curriculum of school work with "man and his work."

I.  Begin by knowing the condition of Europe at the close of the 15th century; printing press, revival of learning, reformation, persecutions, navigation. Observe the order.

II.  Effect of these upon explorations and settlement.

### PERIOD OF DISCOVERY.

III.  Spanish.  1. Spanish history, unification of Spain, Ferdinand and Isabella, Moors.

Study the lives of
*Columbus and *Ferdinand de Soto.

| | |
|---|---|
| Ponce de Leon | 1512. |
| Balboa | 1513. |
| *Menendez | 1565. |
| Espejo | 1582. |

(* Give special study.)

IV.  English—
Deal with the English history of this period—Henry VII., Henry VIII., and Elizabeth.

Study the lives of Raleigh, Drake, and the Cabots.

| | |
|---|---|
| V.  Humphrey Gilbert, | 1579. |
| Frobisher, | 1576. |
| Gosnold, | 1602. |

Frobisher and the gold excitement.

Deal with the Mound Builders and the Indians. These have been studied to some extent in the lower grades.

VI.  Correlative Literature.
1.  "Ulysses and Columbus."—Alfred Dale.

Good for facts and style.

2.  "Voyage of Columbus."—S. Rodgers.
    Full of interest.
3.  Extracts from "Prescott's Conquest of Mexico."
    Make careful selections, having in mind facts of correlative advantage.
4.  Help's "Spanish Conquest of America."

## NUMBER. ARITHMETIC.

### Introduction.

The year's work includes measurements and the most practical applications of percentage.

These truths have been considered in dealing with the outlines:

1.  That pupils must first understand how to use figures—the
mechanical part of numbers.

2.  That pupils can then solve all such problems as come within
the realm of their experiences.

3.  That pupils should not be allowed to grapple with problems
that they cannot apply *at once* in practical illustrations.

4.  That pupils need more knowledge along the lines of business
and fewer "nuts to crack".

5.  That following text-books and making them the "basis of all
supplies" is a dangerous method.

What advantage is it to a boy to know how to solve a problem in
bank discount, if he cannot see a practical use of the principle?
Does he know what a bank is?   Could he enter one and do business?
Does he know what conditions must exist in order to warrant such a
problem ?   Try him.

Common Fractions.

Review the mechanical processes until the pupils can get results
in the shortest and plainest manner possible.

Have the children learn early that quick results cannot be obtained if a system of rules must be strictly adhered to.   Because we
may reduce to common denominators when dividing 6⅝ by 2⅓, it does

not follow that we would do the same when dividing $5\frac{1}{2}$ by $2\frac{1}{2}$, for, see:

$$2\frac{1}{4} \mid 5\frac{1}{4}$$

$$\begin{array}{c|c} 2 & \frac{1}{4} \\ \hline & \frac{1}{2\frac{1}{4}} \end{array} = \tfrac{1}{4} \times \tfrac{2}{9} = \tfrac{1}{8}.$$

The pupil will see that $2\frac{1}{4}$ is the result without doing all the work on the board.

$$12\tfrac{8}{9} \div 5 = 2\tfrac{78}{45}.$$

Process:     $5 \mid 12\tfrac{8}{9}$

$$\begin{array}{c|c} 2 & 2\tfrac{8}{9} \\ \hline & \frac{}{5} \end{array} = \tfrac{76}{45}.$$

It is fallacious to allow pupils to write out full processes, even at first. The earlier a child does away with long written-out processes, the sooner will he see quick and correct results. The exact mind never thinks slowly. You seldom see slow thinkers *exact* in numbers.

After the children can master the mechanical part of fractions, introduce simple problems; as—

There are $25\frac{1}{2}$ bu. in one bin, $83\frac{3}{4}$ bu. in another, and $17\frac{3}{10}$ bu. in another; if I put them equally into two bins, how many bu. in each?

Process.     $25\frac{1}{2}$ bu.
　　　　　　 $83\frac{1}{4}$ "
　　　　　　 $17\frac{3}{10}$ "

$$2 \mid 126\frac{1}{4} \text{ bu.}$$
　　　　　　 $63\frac{1}{8}$ bu.   Ans.

Correlate the questions with the other branches—geography, history, using the day's lesson for a basis in arithmetic. Suppose the West Indies is the subject in geography to-day.

Questions.

1.  The area of the West Indies is 94,398 sq. mi., Mass. has 8,315 sq. mi. How many states equal to Mass. would the W. Indies make?

2.  Cuba produces $1\frac{7}{8}$ bbls. of molasses to the acre, Porto Rico, $1\frac{3}{4}$ bbls., Haiti, $1\frac{2}{3}$ bbls., and Jamaica, $1\frac{1}{2}$ bbls.; what is the average yield per acre?

Draw the islands—the drill will be beneficial.

## LANGUAGE.  ENGLISH.

### Introduction.

The pupils have had careful drill up to this time on writing sentences.  The chief points kept in mind for the year are:
1. A correct use of English.
2. A fluent use of English.
3. A practical use of it.
4. How to know when right.

This involves, how to know when the English is correct or wrong; hence comes a careful study of construction.  But why learn the use of language alone?  why not weave in our literature, science, history, etc.?

Children will not object if a written lesson be assigned on "Grand Pre and its people," after they have carefully read Evangeline, but they would rebel if asked to write an *essay* on "Conduct," "Spring," "Innocence" and the "rest."

We are always anxious to learn other people's opinion of things.

What Shakespeare thought of "Mercy," in the lines beginning—

"The quality of mercy is not strained,
It droppeth as the gentle rain from heaven
Upon the place beneath:" etc.,

is a revelation to us: we see kindness differently.  It is thus with all good literature.  It enlightens and vivifies every branch in the school curriculum.

1. Synthesis.

(*a*)  Begin by building sentences with unmodified subject and predicate.  Lead the pupils to see the two parts—subject and predicate.  Choose examples from the readers, histories, etc., to illustrate.  Teach them to see that name and noun mean the same, and "doing or being" words are called verbs.  Later, modify the subject and predicate but do not call attention to the modifiers.

(*b*)  Review the three kinds of sentences with respect to use—declarative, interrogative, and imperative.  Show that the exclamatory sentence is a peculiar form of any one of the other three.

(*c*)  Noun.  Make lists, being careful to include all kinds.  Classify into common and proper.  Emphasize the writing of both, and teach punctuation from the very beginning. Do *not* accept work not well punctuated. Note how nouns may change classes. Classify nouns (common) into class nouns, abstract, collective and verbal. Readers will supply large lists. Teach some of the easy properties, such as gender, person and number. Syntax can be left until more of the sentence is mastered. Review forming plurals, and nouns denoting ownership. Drill on common expressions. Give board drill.

Plurals of Nouns
1. Most nouns form their plurals by adding "s" to the singular.
2. "f" and "fe" rule.
3. When "es" instead of "s"?
4. Change of word—tooth, mouse, etc.
5. "Y" rule { (*a*) When a consonant precedes. (*b*) When a vowel precedes.
*Master these completely.*

(*d*)
Ownership Nouns. How written.
1. Adding the apostrophe and "s" to singular nouns.
2. Adding the apostrophe *only* to a *plural* noun ending in "s".
3. Adding the apostrophe and "s" to a *plural* noun *not* ending in "s".
Teach that ownership is often expressed by the "of" phrase
Account for the origin of the apostrophe to denote ownership.

(*e*) Pronoun. Teach that the pronoun must fill the office of its antecedent, the noun. Bring this out plainly by building sentences. Search reader for kinds of pronouns. Classify list into personal, relative and interrogative. Study the personal, and leave the other classes until the adjective clause is taken up. Emphasize the forms. Criticize the language of the pupils, also their composition with reference to correct use of pronouns in the predicate.

(*f*) Verb. Uses—form lists from some familiar selection. Classify into transitive and intransitive, regular and irregular. Observe the number of the verb when used in sentences.

Keep clear of book definitions. Do not teach a fact that will not lead to the next step. Much must be omitted during the first few months, that may be taken up later when the pupils will have mastered the primary sentence. Base all English upon composition work. Remember, after all, true English is writing and speaking the language correctly and elegantly. Science, history and literature present excellent material for composition.

Interesting subjects in September work : "Indians," "Columbus in Europe," "Life in the Atlantic," "Spanish Customs."

## THE ARTS.

### Introduction.

Under the arts are put writing, music, drawing, and miscellaneous work. While some of the last do not rightfully come under this head, yet this period must include much that otherwise would find no place, and yet means so much to a course of study.

Children in this grade have learned the correct form of letters, and require constant drill and exercise in acquiring an easy, rapid hand. No written work should be accepted unless the mechanical work has been carefully executed

The pupils have had considerable drill in reading music, hence special attention can be given to tone forming, enunciation, and intonation. Only a few songs have been suggested. The pupils always have some favorites they wish to sing. Do not wait for a particular time for singing but embrace the opportune minute when the children are tired and interest lags; then have them rise, throw up the windows, throw off care, and sing, sing.

The special work on Masters of Painting will be found very interesting. The author has tried this line of work and found that the keenest interest was manifested by the pupils.

But deal with the artists as real men. Don't give lectures. Have plenty of pictures (copies) before the school. The Perry Co., Malden, Mass., publishes excellent copies of great paintings at cheap prices. Get a hundred and mount them on bristol board for the school-room. The cost will be slight. Our American schools are overlooking the value of this branch of the fine arts. Why not create an interest in fine paintings in our public schools ? How many children, and adults too, have never heard of Raphael's Sistine Madonna, Millet's Angelus, etc. ?

I.  Writing.

Let vertical writing be used in all written work. Require the pupils to do their best not only during the period for practice, but at all times. Do not accept inferior writing on the board, or in Ms.-work. Be careful that no other system is used by either the teacher or the pupils.

Have daily, periods for practice in writing, keeping in mind correct forms, and speed.     Do not allow pupils to fall into a slow way. Require rapid work.   Cultivate ease of movement.

II.   Music.

Have singing every day.

Spend some time in reading exercises.

See that the pupils sing naturally and with ease.   Keep the music within proper register.   Pitching songs too high is a common mistake.

The average voice of children cannot reach above "D" with any ease.

Choose songs with melody and sentiment.    Annie Laurie is liked by all children.    It makes a beautiful two part song.    The sentiment is good.   Teach the conception of the words.

Grandmother's Chair is full of melody and contains a wholesome lesson.

Do not drag the song—cut the words off—make the utterance distinct.

III.   Drawing.

Materials,—*Models:* Equilateral triangular prism—cylinder—oval ellipse; boxes, baskets, fruits and flowers.

Points in representation:

    1.   Drawing objects level,—above, and below the eye.

    2.   Distance between the observer and the object.

    3.   Distance influences apparent size.

    4.   Position influences apparent form.

Decoration

    1.   Geometric units in decorative arrangement.

    2.   Conventionalized leaf units.

    3.   Original work.

Sketching.

Simple views—trees—landscapes—houses—trains.

## NATURE STUDY.

A study of 25 common weeds.

Make out the list so as to include the most common.   Allow the children to gather them, root, stems, and flowers and note carefully:

1. Height.
2. Kind of leaves.
3. Infloresence.
4. Roots.
5. Peculiarities.
6. Habitat.

Observe how each kind sows its seed and how else propagated. Study the uses made of some of the common weeds, such as pepermint, etc. Teach some appropriate literature with the subject. Have the weeds gathered, carefully pressed and mounted on white card board, or drawing paper, writing below the mounted specimen: (1) common name, (5) when it blooms, (3) habitat, and some literature appropriate.

# OCTOBER, or Second Month.
## GEOGRAPHY.

I.  NORTH AMERICA.—APPALACHIAN HIGHLAND.
    1.  Direction and slopes.
    2.  Ranges of mountains—effect upon climate.
    3.  Western slope—Ohio R. and branches.
    4.  Climate—rain fall.
    5.  Productions ⎰ Mineral. ⎱ Vegetable. ⎰ Animal.
    6.  Cities, rivers, points of interest.

Keep in mind size and direction from us.    It is well to have pupils point the direction of places as they answer, and also give a fair estimate of distance; e. g.:  Mt. Mitchell is S. W. (here let pupils point) and about 300 miles from California, Pa.  The best results are obtained from this kind of drill.    The children do not memorize answers to questions but reason by measuring and thinking out positions.

Teach geography by comparison—consider places from a home standpoint.

Keep a large arrow marked on the floor with  chalk, showing directions.

II.  MISSISSIPPI R. BASIN.
    1.  Size and shape—have it sketched.
    2.  Slopes—how they affect climate, productions, etc.
    3.  Tributaries—how fed.
    4.  Amount of erosion—silt—growth of coastal plain.
    5.  Levees, crevasses.
    6.  Productions, why rice and sugar in the South.
    7.  Cities, caves, battle-fields, etc.

Have pupils understand the size of the Mississippi R.—its length, average width—low water, floods—amount of silt carried each year, how the hills here are being flattened and the soil carried  to build up the coastal plain.  Why levees must be built along the  lower  course of the Mississippi R. and not along other rivers.  Size of the levees, how built, who pays expense.

Draw a cross section of  the river  showing the bed and adjoining country.

Show how Vicksburg is rapidly becoming an inland city.  Rivers

with great curves indicate what? St. Francis lowlands once the bed of
the Mississippi R.

    Illustrate a typical plantation.

    Keep in mind direction and distance from pupil's home.

III.  St. Lawrence R. and the Great Lakes.

    1.  Extent of territory drained.

    2.  Size, shape and relative position of the lakes.

    3.  How fed.  Banks of the St. Lawrence.

    4.  Straits, rapids, falls, islands.

    5.  Cities and commerce--Erie Canal.

Emphasize the amount of produce carried by this route.  Where
obtained.  Growth of Chicago, and other lake ports.  Time of traveling from the mouth of the St. Lawrence to Duluth.  Fish industry.

------------

## NATURE STUDY.

Study of leaves.

    Make a collection of 25 leaves.  Have them pressed and care-
ufflly mounted on cardboard 8x10 inches.  Below each leaf mounted,
write this data:

    1.  Kind.

    2.  Shape.

    3.  Size.

    4.  Venation.

    5.  Arrangement.

Study the form and draw each leaf.

    Make blue prints of the leaves and be careful to show perfectly
formed specimens.  Large compound leaves may be printed on paper
much larger, or else choose smaller specimens and note the fact.  Correlate history and geography with nature study.  Elm leaves, suggest
the Quaker Elm.  Oak, suggest the Charter Oak, etc.

------------

## U. S. HISTORY AND LITERATURE.

French.

    I.  Study Francis I. and his dealings with Verrazani, also include

La Salle, the work of the Jesuit Missionaries and the Huguenots.

    II.    Cartier,               1535.

             Ribaut,              1562.

             Champlain (twice)    1605–8.

             Du Monts,           1605.

    Tell what each did.  Spanish Massacre.  Dutch.  Life of Henry Hudson.

    III.    Sum up the claims of the four nations and have the pupils know upon what discoveries each nation based its claim.  Construct maps showing the claims of each nation.  This can be done by making a map for *each* nation's claims.  Color the claims.  Morris' History of the U. S. gives some good suggestions concerning this.

Correlative Literature.

      1.   "LaSalle and the Discovery of the Great Lakes."—Parkman.

           Read all if possible.  It is excellent.

      2.   "The Paper Canoe."

           A short description of a trip down the Mississippi R. in La Salle's time.

      3.   "Jesuits in North America."—Parkman.

## ARITHMETIC.

MEASUREMENTS.  SURFACE.

    I.    Analyze the linear and square tables, then have them memorized.  Never leave a table until every pupil knows it as well as he knows his multiplication table.  It is interesting to the children to know why the yard has three ft., the rod $16\frac{1}{2}$ ft., etc.  Teach them this. Teach square measure by actually measuring.

    II.    Carpeting.

    First teach matching of carpet (can illustrate with wall paper), waste, laying in strips, turning under.

    Have pupils measure the school-room, calculate the number of yards by laying the carpet either way.

    Measure irregularly shaped rooms and compute the carpet for them.  Use different widths of carpet.  *Have the diagrams accompany each computation.*

    III.    Plastering.

    Observe the openings, number of coats, ceiling, *current prices* for work.

IV.  Painting.

See plastering and carpeting.  Have children carpet, plaster, and paint some room in the building,—each measuring for himself.  Use current prices.

------

## LANGUAGE

Phrases.  Teach that the place of an adjective or adverb may be filled by a phrase; hence the adjective or adverb phrase; e. g.: A *strong* man=A man *of strength*.  He traveled *northward* =He traveled *toward the north*.

Notice that the adjective goes *before* its noun, generally; but the adjective phrase goes *after*.  Emphasize these cardinal points.

1.  Modifiers of nouns and pronouns are adjective elements, and may be words, phrases, or clauses.

2.  Modifiers of verbs, adjectives, and adverbs are adverb elements, and may be words, phrases, or clauses.

Give daily drill in the following synthetic work :

1.  Flowers bloom.—Unmodified.

2.  *Beautiful* flowers bloom *profusely*.   Modified sentences— *words*, adj. and adv.

3.  Flowers *of the forest* bloom *during the night*.  Modified sentences.  *Phrases*, adj. and adv.

4.  *Many* flowers *of the forest* bloom *frequently during the night*.  Modified sentences.  *Words and phrases*, adj. and adv.

If the pupils grasp the construction readily introduce the adj. and adv. clause.

5.  *Many* flowers *of the forest* *which last but a few hours* bloom *frequently* *during the night* *when it is cool*.  Modified sentence.  Words, phrases, and clauses, adj. and adv.

If this kind of work is continued daily for the month, growing gradually into more complex constructions, the hardest battle of grammar will have been fought, and without drudgery.

Children delight in *using* language but dislike the memorizing of definitions, etc.

For interesting and profitable work allow 12 line compositions to be written, first with unmodified sentences, then with No. 2, then No. 3, 4, and 5.  Have the best copied on the board for special criticism.

Continue composition work as suggested for September.

## THE ARTS.

I. Writing.

See work for September.    Continue the same, demanding neat and rapid work.

II. Music.

Drill on music reading, introducing part work.    Be careful in introducing changes of key in the same exercise.    Take simple changes first; as: C to F; Eb to Ab.

"October Party" is a very appropriate song for this season of the year.    It is sometimes called "November's Party," found in "The Model Music Course"—John Church Co.

"The Little Brown Church in the Dale" is a favorite with most pupils of this grade.    Endeavor to sing the chorus with all parts.

In singing observe:

1. Correct tone.
2. Proper breathing.
3. Distinct enunciation.
4. Proper position (standing).
5. Cadences.

# NOVEMBER, or Third Month.

## GEOGRAPHY.

I. NORTH AMERICA—WESTERN HIGHLAND.
   1. Extent.
   2. Mountains
{
      Rocky.
      Wahsatch.
      Sierra Nevada, Cascade.
      Coast Range.
}
   3. Great Basin.
   4. California Basin.
   5. River valleys and plateaus.
   6. Wealth, rain fall.
   7. Climate—how affected.
   8. Parks, Indian reservations.
   9. Rivers, cities, arms of the ocean, etc.

Compare the Western Highland with the Eastern Highland in size, surface, climate and productions. Compare the Appalachian with the Rocky mountains. Why so many large parks and high peaks? Make a careful study of them. Canons—how formed, why so numerous? How can we determine the age of the rivers? Use plenty of number work with the geography. It will add to the interest. Compare latitude of California with Pennsylvania. Why is the climate so different? Salmon fisheries of the Columbia.

Golden Gate, big trees, classes of people, industries, products.

II. PRAIRIE AND PLAIN REGIONS.
   1. Extent.
   2. Causes of prairies.
   3. American desert—causes.
   4. Industries.
   5. Western farming, and cow-boy life.
   6. Cities, rivers, mountains, etc.

Treat of the early history of the Prairie,—how broken up—grasses—kind of soil—animals—industries—Indian occupations. Picture the cow-boy life on the plains. Do him justice. Remember some culture exists among the rough (?) boys of the plains.

Irrigation—artesian wells—the American desert becoming an English garden.

Modern machinery used in the farming country.    Read extracts from "The Prairie" to pupils.  Have plenty of pictures.  Causes of western emigration.

III.    REVIEW RELIEF FORMS OF NORTH AMERICA.

Have much written work.

Require pupils to go to the board and sketch a basin, or slope, in say three minutes.  Arouse competition in exactness and neatness of work.  Have pupils construct relief maps from memory—hang up for exhibition.

## NATURE STUDY.

NUTS.

Make a collection of nuts.

    1.    Those about home.

    2.    Those not about home but native to the U. S.

    3.    Foreign nuts.

Collect and arrange in shallow paper boxes, similar to a mineral collection.

Study each kind and label.  Draw some of them on the outside of the boxes, or on paper and then paste.  Study the mode of cultivating, nature of plants and trees producing.  Carefully note the time and manner of gathering.  How marketed and current prices.

## U. S. HISTORY AND LITERATURE.

Period of Settlement.

I.    London and Plymouth Companies.

Teach the organization, the territory embraced in each, the territory intervening.    Why ?    Locate the boundary parallels upon the maps, showing the claims of the nations.

Sir George Popham's attempt to settle at the mouth of the Kennebec, Me. The same year Jamestown was founded by the London Company.

II.    Get a general knowledge of English history during this period.

James I., Charles I., Cromwell, Charles II., James II., William and Mary, and Anne.

III.    Virginia.

Jamestown—government, education, etc.

John Smith Story.
Famine.
Assembly.
Indian Troubles.
Charters.
Navigation Acts.
Bacon's Rebellion.

Make John Smith the historic center.

IV.   Massachusetts.

Two leading settlements.

1.   PLYMOUTH COLONY—PURITANS:

(*a*)   Origin (Milton and Cromwell), wanderings in Europe.   (*b*)   Landing of the Pilgrims—their first winter—treaty with the Indians.   (*c*)   Miles Standish, growth of colony, government.

2.   MASSACHUSETTS BAY COLONY.  (BOSTON).

(*a*)   Settlement—character of settlers.

(*b*)   Religious disturbances $\begin{cases} \text{Roger Williams.} \\ \text{Anne Hutchison.} \\ \text{Quakers.} \end{cases}$

(*c*)   Salem Witchcraft and other delusions.

(*d*)   Schools—industries.

3.   King Philip's War.

4.   Union of Colonies—Cause.

5.   Prominent men $\begin{cases} \text{Thomas Hooker.} \\ \text{Roger Williams.} \\ \text{Miles Standish.} \\ \text{Cotton Mather.} \end{cases}$

6.   Trace the influence of these two colonies up to the present time. Treat Rhode Island (Williams, charter), New Hampshire (Mason),and Connecticut (Andros, Charter Oak),as foster colonies of Massachusetts.

Correlative Literature.

1.   "Courtship of Miles Standish."—Longfellow.
      Beautiful and realistic.

2.   "First Landing of the Pilgrims."—Southey.
      A piece of fine literature.

3.   "The Mayflower" and "The Phantom Ship."
      Both gems of verse.

4.   "Heartbreak Hill."
      Children admire it.

## ARITHMETIC.

MEASUREMENTS.  CAPACITY.

Analyze the tables of capacity—then memorize as in the work for October.  Such numbers as 231 cu. in. in a gal., 2150.42 cu. in. in a bu. (stroked), etc., must be acquired.  Teach the origin of the bu., qt., gal., hhd., etc.  This is generally overlooked, but it should not be so, or arithmetic will be working with figures alone.

Use parallelopiped figures at first, then take up the curved ones. Review the circle, circumference, area, etc.

Compute the capacity of your rooms, vessels in the room, your cistern.

Correlate with the science.

Continually introduce questions that will involve careful work in a mechanical way.

Insist upon neat and exact drawing of figures.  Let not a problem be accepted that does not have its diagram.

## LANGUAGE.

PROPERTIES.

I.  Continue the work of the previous month and introduce the properties of the noun, adjective, adverb.  Deal with the preposition and classify.  Emphasize the use of prepositions with particular words —choice of prep.  Introduce the interjection and show how conjunctions connect words, phrases and clauses.  Have each case illustrated. Do not be satisfied with one illustration but call up the points daily.  Introduce the participle and infinitive.  Show the uses of each in short sentences, as was explained in October work.  Emphasize the *noun* use of the infinitive.

II.  Give daily work in analyzing simple sentences.  Be careful in choosing them.  In assigning work for the next lesson, see that the sentences are from standard authors—many will do for memory gems. Give plenty of work in paraphrasing.  Begin with easy selections. Require neat Mss.  Watch the spoken language, introduce rules of syntax when advantageous.

verb, don't burden them with a rule.

Make the compositions short—one or two pages are sufficient

Teach the pupils to be methodical in thought.   Observe paragraphing. Be sure to indent when beginning a paragraph.  Paraphrase selections from "Miles Standish" and "First Landing of the Pilgrims."  Have pupils read their work in class for criticism.

## THE ARTS.

I.   WRITING.

Write business forms—such as the different kinds of notes, receipts, etc.

II.   MUSIC.

Memorize some of the most common hymns and national songs. We should all know by heart more of these common hymns.   Teach: "Jesus, Lover of My Soul," "Nearer, My God, to Thee," "Rock of Ages," "All Hail the Power of Jesus' Name," "Just as I Am," "Home Sweet Home," "America," etc.

III.   DRAWING.

Different kinds of nut trees; observing size of stem, branches, leaves, and fruit.

# DECEMBER, or Fourth Month.
## GEOGRAPHY.

I.   NORTH AMERICA—United States.

    U. S. { Government. / Climate. / Grouping of States. / Products.

1.  Government of U. S.

Legislative
- Representatives { Number? / By whom elected? / Term? / Qualifications—Salary.
- Senators { Number? / By whom elected? / Qualifications? / Salary? / Term?

Executive
- President. Vice Pres. { Term? / By whom elected? / Qualifications? / Salary of Judges?
- Cabinet. (Art. II., Sec. 2. cl. 2.) { Secretary of State. / " " Treasury. / " " War. / " " Navy. / " " Interior. / " " Agriculture. / Postmaster General. / Attorney General.

Judicial. (Art. III., Sec. 1. Art. II., Sec. 2, cl. 2.)
- Supreme Court { Term of Judges? / 1 Chief Justice. / 8 Associate Judges.
- Circuit Courts. { Term? / One Judge in each court.
- District Courts. { Term? / One Judge in each district.
- Court of Claims { Term? / Five Judges.

Do not attempt too much.    Present the subject in a simple and illustrative way.   For example show pictures of public buildings, halls of congress, &c.

2.  Climate.

Review the causes that affect climate, and how parts of the U. S. are affected by one or more.

Causes that affect climate. {
Latitude.
Altitude.
Ocean Currents.
Distance from Sea.
Winds (prevailing).
Vegetation.
}

3.  Grouping of States

Classify the states into 10 groups, according to Harper.   While there are some disadvantages in this grouping, there are advantages far greater.

Study each group, observing the following outline, or one equivalent.

Middle Atlantic States {
Position.
Area.
Surface.
Climate.
Industries.
Mountains.
Rivers.
Lakes.
Cities.
Bays.
Capes.
Special facts.
}

Use relative terms in describing the area, climate and surface.

Have the groups drawn on the board large enough to be seen by the whole school.

Connect interesting data with as many places as possible; e. g,:

Chautauqua—Assembly; Catskill—"Sleepy Hollow"; West Point --Military School, etc.

4.  Products.

Construct product map.

Do not make it smaller than 3x5 feet.   Draw outline of states on it and place on products with Royal glue.   Let the pupils do all this work. Use small phials for material that cannot be fastened otherwise

## NATURE STUDY.

ROCKS.

I. First study the rocks of Vermont and vicinity, including the granite, marble and sandstone. Study the composition, and prove with simple experiments.

Treat at length where found, how quarried, and how marketed. Uses of the different rocks.—Suggestive subjects:

Polishing rocks.

Carving and sawing.

II. Study the cliffs of the Hudson R,, observing veins, and formation.

III. Make a careful study of the different rocks found around home and make a collection of them. Label each specimen and arrange in a cabinet. Allow the children liberty in shaping and arranging their specimens. Correlate literature with the work.

## U. S. HISTORY AND LITERATURE.

Period of Settlement (continued).

I. NEW YORK.

1. Dutch—Make "Irving's Knickerbocker" the basis of history. Study Dutch customs, patroons, four Dutch governors, Swedes, and settlements.

2. English; Duke of York, conquest, Andros, Leisler.

II. PENNSYLVANIA.

1. Quakers; origin (George Fox), first settlements. William Penn, his purpose, charter, Indians, Philadelphia, customs, industries, prominent men.

2. A brief sketch of the history of Pennsylvania to the present time.

3. Foster colonies: New Jersey (Carteret, Presbyterians), Delaware (Swedes).

4. Account for the northern boundary of Delaware, Mason and Dixon's Line and the northwest neck of Pennsylvania. Such little facts are like dessert after the heavy meal.

III. The Carolinas and Maryland are foster colonies of Virginia.

THE CAROLINAS.

    1.    Albemarle and Clarendon colonies.   How settled, Grand Model, John Locke.

    2.    Rice and indigo, divisions of the Carolinas. Indian troubles.

IV.    MARYLAND.  
- The principle of toleration.
- Catholics—history of same.
- Lords Baltimore.
- Religious freedom.
- The Clayborne troubles.
- William and Mary on the throne of England.
- Changes.

    V.  GEORGIA.

    1.    Oglethorpe's project, imprisonment of debtors, kind of settlers, Georgian industries, restrictive laws.

    2.    The Wesleys and Whitefield, home for the poor, troubles with Spain.

Correlative Literature.

    1.    "Irving's Knickerbocker's History of New York."

    2.    "Van Rensselaer of Rensselaerswick."—Brook.

        (Humorous and entertaining.)

    3.    "Historic Boys."

    A careful study of Irving will add much interest to the month's work.

---

## ARITHMETIC.

MEASUREMENTS.   WEIGHT.

    Study carefully avoirdupois, troy, and apothecary weights.   Deal with the origin of the terms.   Why 24 gr. = 1 pwt.?   Why 8 fluid dr. = 1 fluid oz.?  Notice that the troy and the apothecary weights are the same in lb., oz., and gr., but that the oz. is differently divided. Compare these two weights with avoirdupois.   Firmly fix 5760 gr. and 7000 gr.   Make a judicious use of the scales.   Have each pupil weigh articles and compute their value.   Use groceries, jewelry, medicines. Avoid theory as much as possible.

    Study the abbreviations and symbols thoroughly.   Make out prescriptions, using the apothecary's terms.   Notice their peculiarities. Why?   Relate some of the wierd stories of ancient alchemists.

    Deal with time measure very much as directed above.   Explain the division of time in former centuries.

Teach the cause of leap-years. Difference between lunar and calendar months. Teach the naming of the months, also the days.

There may be time in this month to teach the other tables, such as cubic, etc. The children are supposed to know the money tables and also the surveyor's table. These can be reviewed as questions are introduced.

Continue to correlate the number work with the science, etc.

Questions and examples.

1. If the government should authorize that the standard weight of a bu. of wheat be 56 lbs., what would I lose, in bu., in selling the wheat from a full bin 4 ft. long, 3 ft. wide, and 5 ft. high?

2. The Rocky Mt. states yield $60,000,000 of silver yearly. What would be the weight of the silver, supposing it was in coin—alloy counting nothing?

Frame the question so as to involve as many new principles as possible. What must the pupil know in the second question? Let us analyze:

      1. Weight of a silver dollar.
      2. Fineness of a silver dollar.
      3. No. oz. in a lb. of silver, etc.

What lines of thought would he likely follow?

      1. Why put alloy in coin?
      2. Why have the silver dollar weigh so many gr.?
      3. Could dollars be used as weights for a balance?
          etc.

Give plenty of work in reduction of denominate numbers.

---

## LANGUAGE.

Special drill on Verbs and Pronouns.

1. Take up the properties of the verb—voice, mode, tense, person, and number. Show why intransitive verbs cannot have voice. Reason it out with the children. Make a scheme of the verb, large enough to be seen across the room, and keep it before the pupils constantly. Show why there are but four tenses in the potential mode. Why one tense and one person in the imperative, etc. Look after the reasons—grammar is not to be memorized. *Text-books are very misleading at times.*

In conjugating a verb in the 3rd, singular, give the three genders of the pronoun.   Drill on the correct use of lie, lay, sit, set, teach, do, shall and will, may and can, stop and stay.

2.    Make a plan of the pronoun showing the case forms in the different persons and numbers.    Drill constantly on the predicate pronoun.   Call attention to the fact that pronouns do not change to an apostrophe and "s" to denote ownership.    Why?    Avoid the use of "them" for "those".    Deal with the interrogative and relative pronouns.   Distinguishing features of the relative?

3.    Continue the analysis of simple sentences.    Notice carefully such sentences as these—"He told me to go," "I made him angry," "He is tired working all day."

Teach transposition, and select many transposed sentences.

Base the composition work on the literature and history.   Have drawings inserted in the compositions.   Hang them up for criticism.

## THE ARTS.

I.   WRITING.
Copy poetry, observing indentations and punctuation.
II.   MUSIC.
Continue the system of previous months in reading music.

Watch the tone and breathing.—Seek for rapid reading and correct time.   Introduce the beautiful song, "Flow Gently, Sweet Afton."   Teach the Scotch history.   Insist upon clear enunciation and proper intonation.

At Xmas time teach "Merry Xmas".—(Excell.)Study the sentiment.   It is beautiful.
III.   Study of Raphael and his Madonnas.
1.   Home and boyhood.
2.   Florence experiences.
3.   His work in Rome.
4.   Style  three kinds.
5.   Works.
Try to have copies of The Coronation of the Virgin, St. Cecilia, SistineMadonna and the Transfiguration.

# JANUARY, or Fifth Month.
## GEOGRAPHY.

I. BRITISH AMERICA —
   1. Extent and ownership.
   2. How ruled.
   3. Surface, climate, and productions.
   4. Political Divisions cities, rivers.

   Compare Quebec and Ontario in people, customs, products, and surface.

   Mark well the forest and wheat regions, quality of furs, mineral wealth, and railroads. Discuss the Esquimaux, fisheries. Remember that New Foundland is ruled differently, and is an independent colony. Danish America—ownership—theory of its discovery, present condition.

II. ALASKA—
   1. Position and size.
   2. Shape and relief.
   3. How acquired.
   4. How governed.
   5. Industries.
   6. Emphasize mineral developments.

   Keep a well sketched map of Alaska on the board. Study the Yukon valley and the climatic changes. In order to realize its size, consider it 12 times that of New York. Why "land of the mid-night sun"? Draw lines from Mt. Kelly to St. Elias and from Cape Romanzof to Manning Point—Measure them and compare with distance from Pittsburg to Texas - By measuring you will find the Eastern boundary is 2 times the length of Pennsylvania. Have much of this kind of work. It will impress shape and size.

III. CENTRAL AMERICA—
   Treat Central America as you did Mexico. Dwell on the five independent republics—the low form of government—causes of the same. How England rules her one colony. Treat at length, the Nicaragua Canal, productions. Population equal to that of Mass. and Conn.

IV. Draw maps of Canada and other countries, construct lines connecting places, determine distance and compare with places about home.

   Correlate the early French history with Canada, and Dutch history with Hudson Bay.

Draw a map showing the relative position of the West Indies, Bahamas, Bermudas, and the S. E. coast of the U. S.

---

## NATURE STUDY.

THE MOON.

Make a general study of the moon, observing the following points:

1. Size, position.
2. Phases.
3. Distance from the earth.
4. Orbit.
5. Rotation.
6. Physical features.
7. Superstitions.

Have drawings made of the phases.

---

## U. S. HISTORY AND LITERATURE.

ANGLICIZING AMERICA.

I.   This is an era of great importance, since it determined the race of a continent; hence the language, religion, laws and customs of America have grown out of this fruitful epoch.

The first three Inter-Colonial wars had their origin in Europe, hence a critical study cannot be given. King William's War, 1689–97; Queen Anne's, 1702–13; King George's, 1744–1748. The causes may be given and also the chief events in America. It would be well to learn place and terms of each treaty.

II.   Before beginning the French and Indian war, review carefully the English and French claims on American soil.

War. — 1755–63.   Cause.

Five objective points.   Why?

1. DuQuesne.  2. Niagara.  3. Ticonderoga and Crown Point. 4. Quebec.  5. Acadia and Louisburg.

III.   Study the situation of these places and the topography of the country surrounding. Read Parkman for facts. He has best told the story of this war.

IV.   Take for special points of study Washington's Journey, Expulsion of the Acadians (Read Evangeline), Battle of Lake George,

and the Battle of Quebec—Treaty.
> V.   Persons for special study.
>> Queen Anne.
>> King George.
>> Washington.
>> Pontiac.
>> Wolfe and Montcalm.
>> William Pitt.
>> Acadians.

> VI.   Have maps constructed showing positions and marches. Call attention to the historic points near here—such as Braddock's grave, etc.

Correlative Literature.
>> "The Old Regime in Canada."— Parkman.
>> "Montcalm and Wolfe."—Parkman.
>>> Both masterpieces of Inter-Colonial history.
>> "Evangeline."—Longfellow.
>>> A pathetic story of the expulsion of the Acadians.

## ARITHMETIC.

PRACTICAL WORK IN DENOMINATE NUMBERS.
> Take up the work by steps.
>> 1.   Reduction, both ascending and descending.
>> 2.   The four fundamental operations.
>> 3.   Writing the first and second.

Teach the short processes and business operations.   For an example take this question:

Find the number of bu. in a bin 10 ft. long, 8 ft. 6 in. wide, and 5 ft. high.

The long process would be to find the number of cu. in. in the bin and divide by 2150.42.   This should be taught first, but then let the pupils know that by finding the number of cu. ft. in the bin and $\times$ by .8, and adding $\frac{1}{2}$ of 1 per cent. to the result, the answer will be the same.   But explain that .8 of 2150.42 cu. in. = 1720.336 cu. in.   If we add to this $\frac{1}{2}$ of 1 per cent. of it and reject the decimal we obtain 1728 cu. in.   Whenever a short process is used, a lucid explanation should be given.   Taking much for granted spoils the reasoning in this exact science.

Review Longitude and Time. This belongs to geography and should be made use of nearly every day in studying the same. It is expedient to commit the number of miles in a degree of longitude at the equator, then at, say 40° latitude, then 50° latitude. This will assist much in the geography work. Don't commit the table without first reasoning it out. Study arithmetic with a *skeptical mind*, let everything be proved.

You will find good material in January science for problems.

## LANGUAGE.

Verb "to be."

1. Study all the forms of this verb, then notice (*a*) its use in forming the passive voice of transitive verbs, (*b*) its use in forming the progressive form in conjugation, (*c*) its frequency in our language, (*d*) and its misuse.

2. Dwell on the perfect tense of verbs, for in the use of this we find many mistakes. Introduce this suggestion :

When we use *has, had, have*, or any form of the verb "*to be*" with another verb, we use the perfect tense of that verb.

3. Enter more into detail with the clause. By synthesis, develop the three kinds, adj., adv., and noun clause. Account for these expressions: adjective relative clause, adverbial clause of manner, subject clause, object clause. Use these terms so the pupils will become acquainted with the language of grammar.

4. Make "Evangeline" a basis for study of style. Study the rhythm, poetic license, and thought. Many of the sentences can be studied as problems for analysis. Keep in mind the building of a useful vocabulary. Throughout the year, let each pupil set down in a specially prepared book such words as the teacher may suggest; these words to become part of the working vocabulary of the pupils. Frequently review them, and have written tests, say, monthly.

Require essays on different parts of Evangeline, and when finished have each pupil write a report, or criticism on it, not to exceed 500 words.

## THE ARTS.

1. WRITING.

Letter forms, and a drill on forming figures. Special attention given to spacing between words.

II. MUSIC.

Part work—rounds reading from average grade scores. Transposing. Give drills in various keys, requiring rapid work at sight. Demand perfect observance of rests.

Teach the "Old Oaken Bucket." "Make a two part song out of it. Drill carefully on the intonation of the vowels. Cultivate expression by *feeling* the sentiment.

Introduce such a song as "Billy Boy" for a rapid drill.

# FEBRUARY, or Sixth Month.

I. SOUTH AMERICA--
   Study the size and shape, and then take up the reliefs—

| | | | |
|---|---|---|---|
| South America. | Valleys. | Llanos | Size. Why treeless? |
| | | Selvas | Size. How drained? |
| | | Pampas | Size. How drained? |
| | Highlands. | Brazilian—Extent. | |
| | | Guiana Highland—Extent. | |
| | | Andean Plateau | Mountain Ranges. Extent. |

Have a large outline map of South America on the board and construct the river basins and water partings before the class. Locate the great cities, also bays, capes, and tributary rivers. Let the pupils sketch hurriedly the continent, showing the reliefs, separated by differently colored crayon. Let others put in the cities, tributaries, etc. Correlate the history Do not fail to have the pupils read selections from "The Land of the Incas."

---

## NATURE STUDY.

STARS.

   Study twelve constellations. Learn to know them in the heavens.
   Teach some of the ancient myths connected with them.
   Teach planets also. Call attention to the different colors of stars.
   Correlate some of the beautiful literature of our own authors.
   Make maps of the constellations.

---

## U. S. HISTORY AND LITERATURE.

REVOLUTIONARY PERIOD.
   1. Condition of America—(a) education, (b) industries, (c) army.
   2. Causes of war. (a) Indirect. The origin of the colonies pointed toward freedom, love of liberty, laws framed to favor the En-

glish manufacturer and merchant at the expense of the colonist.  Navigation acts.

(b)  Direct.  Taxation without representation, writs of assistance, the stamp act, mutiny act, Boston port bill, first Continental congress.

Revolutionary
War.
1. Action around Boston.
2. Washington from Long Island to Morristown
3. Washington from Morristown to Valley Forge
4. Burgoyne.
5. Greene.
6. Yorktown.
7. Separate Battles.
8. Peace—terms.

After the battles around Boston are studied, the rest of the war
can be studied in *three* campaigns, viz:

Washington's, Burgoyne's, and Greene's.

Washington's
1776.
Long Island—Nathan Hale Story.
Harlem Heights—Retreat.
White Plains—Retreat.
North Castle—British army checked.
Philadelphia—Assisted by the weather.
Trenton—Hessians.

Washington's (con't).
1777-78.
Princeton—Stratagem.
Brandywine—LaFayette.
Germantown—Retreat of both armies.
Valley Forge—Winter Quarters.
Monmouth—Lee's treason.

Burgoyne's.
1777.
Forts Crown Point, Ticonderoga and Edward.
After supplies { Bennington (Betty Stark Story)
{ Fort Schuyler (Tory Boy Story)
Surrender at Saratoga.

Greene's
1781.
Cowpens { Morgan.
{ Tarleton.
Race northward.
Guilford Court-House.
Eutaw Springs.

Battle at Yorktown.

*Treaty.*—Terms.

The battle of Camden, and most of those at the different ports
belong to no particular campaign.

Have each pupil prepare a map of the eastern half of the U. S., and insert the campaigns as studied.    Do not use printed outlines, the pupils need the drill.

*Remember outlines do not constitute history.*    They are good sign-posts— there must be travel between—travel through dales and wood-lands.    Remember no one can teach history and know no more than is found in the ordinary text-books.    Cultivate the art of story-telling. Make history real,—talk with the generals, fight with the soldiers, and weep with the bereaved.

Men to be studied.

| | |
|---|---|
| Arnold (treason). | Cornwallis and Howe. |
| Gates and Schuyler. | Gage and Clinton. |
| Greene and La Fayette. | Tories, traitors. |
| Benj. Franklin. | Patriots. |

Give France credit for her assistance.

Study the Declaration of Independence.

Correlative Literature.

"The Spy."--Cooper.
The best historical novel written in America.
"Declaration of Independence."
To be studied carefully.
"Grandmother's Story of Bunker Hill."—Holmes.
A beautiful description in verse.
"Paul Revere's Ride."—Longfellow.
An exciting episode.

## ARITHMETIC.

PERCENTAGE.

Lead the pupils to know that percentage is nothing new; teach it by common fractions, and also decimals.    Avoid using such terms as base, percentage, rate, etc., until the principles are thoroughly mastered.

Begin at once with problems, do not talk about the *new* subject.

A few hints:

James, which is the most—$\frac{1}{2}$, .5, or 50 per cent. of the pupils here?    If all were here, how many per cent.?    If $\frac{3}{4}$ were here?    What is 75 per cent. of 20 boys?    $\frac{3}{4}$ of 20 boys?    .75 of 20 boys?    What is $\frac{1}{3}$ of 60 chairs?    What per cent. of 60 chairs are 20 chairs?    30 chairs? Drill the class on easy problems like these; do not introduce problems in-volving difficult fractions until the principles are learned.    When new

points are being introduced, use small numbers, those that may be
. grasped by the mind at once.

Lead the pupils into all the so-called *cases* of percentage from the
very beginning. At the outset avoid classifying under rules. As soon
as many questions of the same nature are given the process becomes
mechanical.

Base questions upon home and its surroundings, afterwards upon
the February science and history. The Revolutionary war suggests a
broad field for interesting problems.

## LANGUAGE.

1. Continue the work on clauses. Have the pupils classify all
kinds of clauses, and sub-classify the adverb clauses.

Require much synthetic work; e. g.:

(*a*) Write a sentence having an infinitive phrase used as attri-
bute complement.

(*b*) Write a sentence using (e. g.) "who was here" as an adj.,
then as a noun clause.

(*c*) Make a sentence having an infinitive phrase used as an adj.

Let this kind of drill continue until there is no trouble in making
suitable sentences.

2. Spend much of the time analyzing complex sentences. The
pupils should now be able to analyze ordinary sentences, if the *clause
drill* has been vigorously kept up. Take selections from the literature
and analyze. Diagrams may be used, remembering they facilitate the
operation but are of no value in themselves. Let book reports take the
place of other composition work for the greater part of this month.
Urge each pupil to read at least one good book during the month, and
make a report of say 5 pages on it. Insist that this report be free from
errors in English.

## THE ARTS.

I. WRITING.

Practice on unruled paper.

Write forms of invitations, acceptances, etc.

Cultivate the art of arrangement.

II.   MUSIC.

Continue part work and increase the register.   Avoid loud singing.   Drill on the vowels constantly.

"We'd Better Bide a Wee" is a pretty ballad, and children like it.   The music is the chief feature.   Better words may be selected.

"Crowding Awfully" is a good temperance song, well worth learning.

Sing the national songs frequently.   The children delight to sing of America and her heroes.

# MARCH, or Seventh Month.
## GEOGRAPHY.

I.  SOUTH AMERICA—
    1.  Political Divisions.
    2.  Governments.
    3.  Climate and Products.
    4.  People and Industries.
    5.  Recent Political changes.
    A careful study of the ten republics—first studying them as dependencies of Spain and Portugal during the early part of the 17th century.  Dwell on the three European colonies—wealth of same.
    Make a special study of Brazil—after the following outline.

Brazil {
    Position, size, and form.
    Government—(a) Early, (b) Present.
    Reliefs { Rivers.
             { Mountains.
    Climate—How affected?
    Products { Vegetable.
             { Animal.
             { Mineral.
    People—Classes.
    Customs { Home.
            { State.
    Commerce { Foreign—with whom?
             { Domestic.

II.  Make several drawing lessons from the continent.
    Draw—
                1st,—Reliefs.
                2nd,—Political Divisions.
                3rd,—Make Product Maps.

---

## NATURE STUDY.

THE SUN.
    Study the sun as the source of all light and heat, and hence of all life.
    Note its position in the solar system, and make a map of the eight planets, showing the relative orbits of each.   Emphasize the points of

size, distance from the sun, and orbits.

Outline of further study of sun.

1. What?
2. Size.
3. Distance from the earth.
4. Physical features (sun spots, etc.)
5. Superstitions.

Teach some of the beautiful literature written about this planet, read and commit Everett's description of a sunrise. Have experiments, showing the power of the sun both in light and heat.

## U. S. HISTORY AND LITERATURE.

NATIONAL DEVELOPMENT.

I. Review the Articles of Confederation and the Constitution.

II. Condition of colonists at close of the Revolutionary War— population, industries, domestic life (traveling, money, amusements, mail, etc.), common schools, colleges, arts, etc.

III. Washington's Administration
- Needs of the country
  - Treaties.
  - Finance.
  - Organization of depart-[ments.
- Whiskey Rebellion. [Algiers.
- Trouble with England, France, Spain and Indian Wars.

John Adams' Administration.

Dwell on the condition of the country and the troubles with France. How our envoys were treated; X. Y. Z. despatches. Reasons for enacting the Alien and Sedition Laws. Effect of these laws. Party spirit. Keep cause and effect in mind throughout the national period of U. S. history.

Jefferson's Administration.
- A Democrat.
- War with Tripoli.
- Louisiana Purchase.
- Ohio Admitted.
- Monroe sent to France.
- Lewis and Clark Expedition.
- Burr's Treason.
- Slave-Trade Abolished.
- Foreign Troubles.

This is one of the richest periods in the national development.
Correlative Literature.

> "Washington's Farewell Address."
> Life of Washington.

---

## ARITHMETIC.

PRINCIPLES OF GAIN AND LOSS.

I. Refer to February for suggestions in introducing the subject. Emphasize that the *cost* is a very important consideration in dealing with profit and loss. Get the questions from the stores.

Show how goods are marked, both in plain figures and in letters.

Key for marking.

$$\begin{array}{cccccccccc} 1 & 2 & 3 & 4 & 5 & 6 & 7 & 8 & 9 & 0 \\ t & h & e & & b & o & y & & r & u & n & s \end{array}$$

| h b s |
| e y s |
| $4.00 |

Suppose the tab is put on a pair of shoes, h b s represents the cost, and means by the key $2.40. e y s represents the selling price, and means by the key $3.60. The marking price is $4.00 in plain figures.

A question: How shall a dealer mark shoes that cost him $2.40 so as to fall 10 per cent. and still make 50 per cent?

> 50% of $2.40 = $1.20 Gain.
> $2.40 + $1.20 = $3.60 S. P.
> $3.60 ÷ (100% — 10%) = $4.00 Marking P.

*Prove.*

Make questions requiring the finding of cost and selling price.

II. Deal with agents and their work.

Kinds of agents—commissions charged for different kinds of service. Why? Why does a sewing-machine agent get 25 per cent. and a wool-dealer 2 per cent?

Work out questions about the business transacted by your own agents.

Treat insurance in the same manner.

III. Taxes and Duties.

Trace the school tax from the levy until paid out. Get data from your district and make questions from them. Teach the two kinds of taxes—direct and indirect—outline each.

Duties. Why charged? Kinds; how laid? Study the tariff schedule. Get one from Washington, D. C. Go through a custom-house in imagination with the children. Make out a manifest at

Paris, ship the goods to New York city—"Clear the goods", and ship to destinations. Do all this with the children.

Base your later questions on March history and science. This takes in Hamilton's policy and South American products.

---

## LANGUAGE.

"Snow-Bound."

1. Make "Snow-Bound" the basis work for English during this month.

Study it first as a piece of literature—then choose passages for analysis and rhetorical study. Notice the compound sentences and Whittier's easy style. Let pupils choose some of their art study from this selection—imaginative art.

2. Make a special study of Whittier during this month, following some outline similar to this:

      1. Condition of the U. S. when Whittier wrote.
      2. His parentage and boyhood.
      3. Middle life and writing period.
      4. Later life—productions.
      5. Slavery, Politics.
      6. Style.

Study "Maud Muller," "The Witch's Daughter," "In School-days," and "Songs of Labor."

Use "Maud Muller" for work in paraphrasing.

Let the composition work be on the literature.

---

## THE ARTS.

I. WRITING.

Continue with unruled paper. Practice daily in copying from selections in literature.

II. MUSIC

Part work.

Do not take up much new music each day, except for rapid sight reading. Have plenty of songs. Sing what the children like at times; sometimes old hymns, other times patriotic selections, and again Scotch songs. "Blue Bells of Scotland" is appreciated generally. Try it. If the pupils don't like it, tell its story, then try it again.  Introduce good rounds, and sing with life.

III.    DRAWING.

Do considerable map drawing based upon geography.

Sketch buildings and landscapes.

Allow the pupils to choose their material as  much  as   possible. The interests will vary.    Why not ?    Don't make a boy draw a house if he wants to draw his father's horse.

# APRIL, or Eighth Month.
## GEOGRAPHY.

I. EUROPE.
1. Absolute position.
2. Shape and Size.
3. Political Divisions.
4. Governments.
5. Climate, Industries.

Compare latitude of places in Europe with places in U. S.

Study the reliefs of Europe in three parts, viz: (1) Rivers running north: Petchora, Dwina. Onega, Duna, Vistula, Oder'. (2) Rivers running N. west, and west: Elbe, Weser, Rhine, Seine, Loire, Garonne, Douro, Tagus, Gaudiana, and Guadalquiver. (3) Rivers running S. east: Volga, Don, Dnieper, Dneister, Danube, Po, Rhone, Ebro.

By drawing a line from 63° N. Lat. at Ural Mts. to 50° N. Lat. and 15° E. Long. Greenwich. and one from 50° N. Lat. 15° E. Long. Greenwich, to 37° N. Lat. 7° E Long. Greenwich, then one from 50° N. Lat. and 15° E. Long. Greenwich to the Baltic, the three great slopes will be easy to teach.

The same divisions can be used to teach climate, productions,and other facts. Each slope is peculiar in its climate and productions, and even in its people.

II.  Study each country,observing the same outline as was given for Brazil. Keep in mind the form of government, the race, and industries.

---

## NATURE STUDY.

CLOUDS.

1.  Review the formation of clouds, keeping in mind the distance from the earth, and why different with different kinds of clouds. Classify into three classes—1. Cirrus; 2. Cumulus; and 3. Stratus.

Suggestive questions:

Why are clouds higher on a fine day ?

What countries are the most cloudy ?

What is the size of clouds?

What produces the great variety of shapes?

Do winds absorb clouds altogether ?   How ?
Cause of the red tinge at sunset ?
Cause of cloud motion ?
Cause of red sunrise ? etc., etc.
Experimental work leading to the  spark.    Cause of lightning, kinds, results, and accompaniments.

## U. S. HISTORY AND LITERATURE.

I.   Madison's Administration—War of 1812.
Review the troubles with England.   Grasp the war policy of the administration.   Napoleon's double-dealing.   Indian hostilities.   Cause of the declaration of war.

II.   Study the war, making as centers:   Hull (his cowardice), Harrison, Lake Champlain, Lake Erie, Washington, New  Orleans and the sea.    Account for the one-sided struggle.    Notice the greatest battle (New Orleans) fought on American grounds.   Study the condition of the two armies,   ($a$) in equipment,   ($b$) in numbers,   ($c$) and in bravery.

III.   Peace—treaty, terms; results later.
Trouble with Algiers.   Hartford Convention.   A national bank. Admission of Louisiana, 1812, and Indiana in 1816.

IV.   Men to be studied. —

| | |
|---|---|
| Chas. C. Pickney. | Gen. Jackson. |
| Gen. Harrison. | John Burr. |
| Perry. | Tecumseh. |
| Lawrence. | Francis S. Key. |

V.   1812 aphorisms:
"I'll try, sir."
"Don't give up the ship."
"Remember the Raisin."
"We have met the enemy and they are ours."
"He could not be kicked into a fight."

Read   "Perry's Victory on Lake Erie."—James Percival.
"The Boys of 1812."—J. Russell Soley.

## ARITHMETIC.

Money and Stocks—

Interest- why charged?

I. Interest
- Simple
  - Year Method.
  - Six-percent Method.
  - Sixty-day Method.
- Compound
  - Teach with tables at first.
  - Compute tables afterward.
- Annual
  - Uses.
  - Compare with simple and compound

Teach one method thoroughly, and if possible the three methods outlined. The sixty-day method is undoubtedly the best. Put much time on commercial paper. Include partial payments. Use toy money and have pupils make out notes and borrow from the teacher  count up the notes later and demand payment.

II. Exchange.

Begin by starting to Paris via London with $1000, exchange $300 in London, then $500 in Paris, return to London and come home. Explain each step as you go along. Explain the "Exchange." Have sufficient drill of this kind. Show how premium and discount occur.

Deal with Bills of Exchange (3). Remember domestic exchange is conducted through *drafts*.

III. Banks. Organization- government.
Business of banks. Officers.
Construction of bank furniture.
Dealing with banks.
Certificates.
Checks.

Have a bank in the school-room. Do business as if it were a real one. Teach the boys and girls to be business men and women.

IV. Stocks.

Organize a company—do business, declare dividends, or assessments.

Thoroughly explain the workings of the Stock Exchange. Harper's Magazine '86, will give you excellent articles and illustrations. Study stock quotations in the "dailies". Make out an outline and give each student some stock to watch and schedule each day for two weeks. Explain "bulls" and "bears". Each pupil should be able to deal in stocks when he has finished this subject. Treat *per cent.* as *dollars* and you will obviate much trouble; e. g:

Stocks quoted at 112 pay 6 per cent.
6 per cent. means $6 on a $100 share.

Take time to make the subject clear.    Arithmetic is not mastered by working through books.

## LANGUAGE

Lamb's Tales from Shakespeare.

This will be the basis for English during the month.    The new
feature is the *plot*.    Try to have the pupils gain  strength in their composition work by studying arrangement of facts in Shakespeare's plays.

Once in a week read some of the most beautiful passages from
the original.

Study sentences and especially words.    The word study  should
play no small part in the English during the year.    It is a satisfaction
to know that *"drawing-room"* was once *withdrawing-room*, and meant
a room to withdraw to after meals    Study words—primitive, derivative.

During the month the artist Millet will be studied.    Let much
of this work be reproduced.    That is, a short talk be given one day on
the artist and the pupils reproduce it in writing at school the next day.
Do not allow notes to be taken.    This is excellent memory work.

In studying Millet, have reproductions of his paintings before
the pupils and let them write out the painter's idea as it appears to them.

## THE ARTS.

I.   PRACTICE IN VERTICAL WRITING.

Have periods for special practice on Mondays and  Wednesdays.

II.   MUSIC.

Reading of sacred music from the score.    Teach the beautiful
songs: Gottschalk's "Last Hope," and "St. Hilda".    Cultivate a taste
for good music.

Learn Thompson's "For You and For Me".  Put expression into
this gem.

III.   MILLET.

Make a careful study of this artist.    Treat of his home and surroundings when a boy—his special friends, his leaving home, his first
works.

Style of his art.   Why?

Compare Angelo and Raphael.

Study Millet's "The Angelus," and other paintings. Have copies to show the pupils. Let them bring such pictures as they may have.

# MAY, or Ninth Month.
## GEOGRAPHY.

I.  Study England, the German Empire, France. and the Mediterranean from a historic standpoint.

After the physical facts are well known, and cities, products, etc., have been well learned, collect the history around such centers as Charlemagne, Frederick the Great, Louis XIV., and Queen Bess.

The Abbott History Series will aid much in giving interesting material for the pupils.  Children should acquire a taste now for a more extended reading.  These interesting centers will not fail to awaken even a dull boy to active reading and research.

II.  Have product maps made of each of the countries.  They may be made on drawing paper, say 14 in. square. Lines of distance may be put on the same maps, before the products are mounted.

---

## NATURE STUDY.

Experiments with Oxygen.

What it is,—found in quartz, clay, iron ore, air, etc.

Prepare oxygen—

Chemicals needed :

$\frac{1}{4}$ lb. of potassium chlorate ($K Clo_3$), powdered, cost 5 cents.
½ lb. of manganese peroxide ($M N O_2$), powdered, cost 5 cents.

Apparatus needed:

|   |   |
|---|---|
| 2 one qt. glass cans. | |
| 1 tin pan, holding 3 or 4 qts. | $.05 |
| 1 8-inch glass test tube, | .05 |
| 1 cork to fit test tube, | .02 |
| 2 ft. 3-16 inch glass tubing, | .03 |
| 2 ft. 3-16 inch rubber tubing, | .10 |
| 1 small alcohol lamp, | .20 |

Method:—

Thoroughly mix a table spoon full each of the potassium chlorate and manganese peroxide and put the mixture in the 8-inch test tube.  With a round file bore a hole in the cork large enough to allow the glass tubing to be squeezed in.   Make a scratch on the piece of glass tubing 8 inches from one end and break it off.   Heat and bend this short in the middle to a right angle.   Bend the other piece (18 in. long) to an acute angle of 60° about 4 in. from the end.   Connect these glass tubes by the rubber tubing.   Force the short one through the cork and insert in the test tube.   Put a little water in the pan, fill the two cans level full with water, cover each with a piece of pasteboard and quickly invert and place each in the pan with its mouth downward.   Put the short end of the longer tube under the mouth of one of the cans and apply heat to the bottom of the test tube with the alcohol lamp till the can is filled with oxygen.   Withdraw the glass tube and put it under the 2nd can till filled, or till oxygen ceases to come over.

Precaution—Always remove glass tube from water before withdrawing flame, else water will be forced back into test tube and break it.

Experiments :

When filled take jars from pan and cover with the pieces of paste-board.

I.   Take a splinter of wood, light one end, then blow out, leaving only a spark; thrust it into one of the cans.   It instantly blazes up.

II.   Take a piece of picture frame wire, heat one end, dip it into powdered sulphur, ignite in alcohol flame and lower in the can.   It burns with brilliant flashes.

III.   Wrap a wire around a piece of chalk for a handle, then put sulphur on it, ignite and lower in can.   It burns with a blue flame.

By consulting any elementary text-book on chemistry many interesting and instructive experiments may be made. *Composition of air* and the *flame* will result from these primary experiments.

[Note—The alcohol lamp can be made from a vaseline bottle, with a piece of the glass tubing thrust straight through the cork and a wick drawn through it.   Use wood alcohol; it is cheaper.]

## U. S. HISTORY AND LITERATURE.

I.   Thirty Years of Peace and Progress.

A one-party era.   Account for the revival of peace and prosperity.

II.   Monroe's Administration.

His doctrine—why announced ?   Missouri Compromise—fix boundaries.   A commercial invasion--results.   Jackson in Florida. Tariff question.

II. Public Improvements

- The Cumberland Road.
- (National Pike) Begun in 1806.
- Erie Canal.
- Begun in 1817.

LaFayette's return to the U. S.

Politics.

IV. John Quincy Adams' Administration. "The old man eloquent"—Why unpopular? Divisions in political parties—causes. The tariff problem; death of Adams (John) and Jefferson, July 4, 1826. Removal of the Creek Indians.

Beginning of the "Temperance Movement." Notice a new generation of public men rising. Watch for the next.

Review the growth of slavery from 1619 up to 1829.

V. Study in review the finance system, starting with Hamilton and coming up to Jackson.

VI. Study the lives of these people:

*Monroe*— fought with Washington at Brandywine, Germantown, and Monmouth.

*Henry Clay*—ran three times for the presidency. Secretary of State under Adams (J. Q.).

*John C. Calhoun*—Secretary of War under Monroe—elected vice-president twice, 1824-1828.

*Daniel Webster*—The great American orator.

*Senator Hayne*—Supporter of "Nullification".

References for reading.

Gidding's Exiles of Florida.

Parker's Historic Americans.

Carl Schurz's Henry Clay.

---

## ARITHMETIC.

Review of the Subjects taught during the Year.

Let much of the work be oral and the problems original.

Review thoroughly the subjects of percentage. Have each lesson connect with the preceding and lead to the next. Be guided to some extent by frequent written reviews.

## LANGUAGE.

1. Review the parts of speech.
2. Formulate rules of syntax.
3. Formulate definitions.
4. Study of Murillo and Michael Angelo.

(*a*) In reviewing the parts of speech, ignore all excepting vital points. The pupils should now be able to formulate rules for the correct use of language.

(*b*) Keep up analysis, using "Bingen on the Rhine", and Byron's "Greece".

(*c*) Review the writing of letters, putting special emphasis upon the body of the letter. Good letter-writers are few.

(*d*) Reproduction of work given on Murillo and Michael Angelo will constitute most of the composition work for the month.

## THE ARTS.

I. WRITING.

Have practice every other day. Require pen work in picture study.

II. MUSIC.

Take up some easy cantata and practice it during the month, render it at the close of school. Choose one with choruses principally.

III. MURILLO AND MICHAEL ANGELO.

Study their lives and works.

Outline for Murillo:

1. Place and time.
2. Connection with Castillo.
3. Study of Italian and Flemish art.
4. His marriage—Cadiz.
5. Style—Works.

Outline for Michael Angelo:

1. Place and Time.
2. Parentage.
3. Education.
4. At Bologna.
5. At Rome.

6. Sistine Chapel.
7. St. Peter's.
8. His character.
9. Works.

# Books of Reference.

## FOR BOTH TEACHER AND PUPILS.

*May be used by the pupils.

### GEOGRAPHY.

*In the Trades, The Tropics,and Roaring Forties.—Lady Ann Brassey.
*A White Umbrella in Mexico.—F. Hopkinson Smith.
*Ten Days in Spain.—Kate Field.
*From Yellowstone Park to Alaska.—F. C. Sessions.
*Land of the Midnight Sun.—Du Chaillu.
*Walks in Rome. *Cities of Southern Italy and Sicily, Studies in Rus-
    sia, *Old Country Life.—A. J. C. Hare.
A Journey in Brazil.—Louis Agassiz.
*Views Afoot, and Eldorado.—Bayard Taylor.
*Beyond the Mississippi.—A. D. Richardson.
*A Family Flight Around Home.—E. E. Hale.
*Bits of Travel at Home —Helen Hunt Jackson.
*Glimpses of Three Coasts.—H. H. Jackson.
Spanish American Republics.—Theodore Child.
How to Teach Geography.—E. Carver.
*Stories of Northern Europe, and *Stories of England.—Edinboro Pub.
    Co.
*Geography for Young Folks.—Pratt.
*The Zig-Zag Books.—H. Butterworth.
*Boy Travelers.—Thos. W. Knox.
*Tracing and Sketching Lessons.—S. Y. Gillan.
*Natural Geographies.—J. Redway and R. Hinman.

### U. S. HISTORY.

Parkman's Works.
The Doomed Chief (King Philip) —D. P. Thompson.
Washington and the American Revolution.—Irving.
The Rear Guard of the Revolution.—J. R. Gilmore.
*Short History of English Colonies in America.—H. C. Lodge.
*The Puritan in Holland England—and America.—D. Campbell.
*The Battle Fields of the Revolution.—Thos. Y. Rhoads.
Half Hours with American History.—Charles Morris.
*History of the U. S.—Higginson.
John Fiske's History of the United States.
Adam's History of the U. S.

Flash Lights of American History.—D. C. Murphy.
"Old Glory."—A. E. Maltby.
*Blue Jackets of '61, *Blue Jackets of 1812, *Blue Jackets of 1776.—W. J. Abbott.
*Old Times in the Colonies.—C. C. Coffin.
Building up the Nation.—C. C. Coffin.
*Pizarro.—Mara L. Pratt.
*Raleigh.—Geo. M. Towle.
*Battle Fields and Victory.—W. J. Abbott.
*The Boys of 1812.—J. Russell Soley.
*Young Folk's History of the Civil War.—Mrs. Emma Cheney.
The Old French War.—Rossiter Johnson.
Washington and His Generals.—J. T. Headley.
Alexander Hamilton.—H. C. Lodge.
Henry Clay.—Carl Schurz.
*Patrick Henry.—M. Coit Tyler.
Daniel Webster.—J. Bauvard.
*Benj. Franklin.—J. Chaplain.
*Capt. John Smith.—Gilmore Simms.
*Abraham Lincoln.—Phoebe Hanaford.
*The Century War Book.
*Stories in American History.—Mara L. Pratt.

### ARITHMETIC.

*Number by Grades.—Prince.
Practical Arithmetic.—Wentworth.
Psychology of Number.—McClelland and Dewey.
*Second Lessons in Arithmetic.—H. N. Wheeler.
Mathematical Teaching.—Safford.
Standard Complete Arithmetic.
*The Complete Arithmetic.—Thompson.
*Graded Work in Arithmetic.—Baird.
*Mental Arithmetic.—Milne.
*Brook's Series of Arithmetics.
How to Teach Arithmetic.—Cook.

### LANGUAGE.—ENGLISH.

Language Helps for Teachers.—Sarah L. Arnold.
How to Teach Language.—Metcalf.
*Outlines of English Grammar.—Geo. E. Williams.
*Practical English Grammar.—Welsh.

*Suggestive Lessons on Language.—Badlam.
English in Preparatory Schools.—Huffcutt.
Grammar and Composition.—Lyte.
English Language and Grammar.—Meiklejohn.
*Reed and Kellogg's English Series.
*English Grammar.—Maxwell.
*Language Lessons.—Long.
Composition.—Newcomer.

### ARTS.

*The Old Masters and Their Pictures.—Mrs. Sarah Tytler.
*Legends of the Madonna.—Mrs. Anna Jameson.
Artists of the Nineteenth Century.—Mrs. Clara E. Clement.
A Painter's Camp.—Philip G. Hamerton.
Musical Composers and Their Works.—Mrs. Sarah Tytler.
Memoirs of the Early Italian Painters.—Mrs. Anna Jameson.
Ruskin's Works.
*Sketching from Nature.—T. Rowbotham.
*Figure Drawing.—C. H. Weigall.

### PROFESSIONAL.

Education.—Herbert Spencer.
Lectures on the Science and Art of Education.—Joseph Payne.
Theory and Practice.—Page.
Talks on Teaching.—Parker.
Quincy Methods.—Patridge.
Methods of Instruction.—Wickersham.
White's New Pedagogy —E. E. White.
Educational Reformers.—Quick.
History of Education.—Painter.
History of Pedagogy.—Compayre.
Psychology for Young Teachers.—Hewett.
School Amusements.—Root.
School Management.—Raub.
Waymarks for Teachers.—Sarah L. Arnold.
Philosophy of Arithmetic.—Brooks.
Emile.—Rosseau.
Leonard and Gertrude.—Pestalozzi.
Talks with Teachers.—Mayo.
Evolution of Dodd.—Hawley Smith.
A New Psychology.—W. T. Harris.

www.ingramcontent.com/pod-product-compliance
Lightning Source LLC
Chambersburg PA
CBHW030717110426
42739CB00030B/704